Egyptian Mythology

Gods, Kings, Queens, & Pharaohs

Blake Thomas

Table of Contents

Blake Thomas

Chapter 1

An Introduction to the World of Ancient Egypt

The pharaohs, queens and gods of ancient Egypt have continued to inspire people from all over the world for centuries. Since antiquity, scholars, professionals of all areas and enthusiasts have flocked to Egypt to discover more about this extremely powerful but still mysterious civilization. This book intends to delve into this enigmatic culture, looking at some of the pharaohs, the Egyptian queens and the gods they worshipped.

The ancient kings of Egypt were known as '*pharaohs*', a term which has been used for centuries still. The origin of this title is credited to the Hebrew pronunciation of the Egyptian word *per-aa*, which can be translated as Big House, referring to the royal dwelling. As time went on, it began to be applied to the king himself. When a pharaoh took the throne, he was presented with five names that created his titulary. These included his Horus name, the Two Ladies name, the Gold Falcon name, the son of Ra name (his birth name) and the King of Upper and Lower Egypt name (throne name). The throne and birth names were encircled in a cartouche when inscribed.

The pharaoh and the office of the monarch were seen as the center of the Egyptian culture. It was the pharaoh's job to ensure that he maintained the status quo regarding societal order, known as *ma'at*. Included in this were political stability, maintaining peace and order, dispensing justice, overseeing the economic balance, appeasing the gods through sacred rituals and safeguarding the country from both domestic and foreign threats.

The pharaoh has often been considered as a divine being – as the living representation of the gods on earth. In reality though, it was the power of the kingship that the pharaoh symbolized, which was considered divine, not the actual pharaoh himself. Living pharaohs were linked with the god Horus, whereas deceased pharaohs were associated with Osiris (we shall look into both these gods and their stories in detail in the following chapters), but the common people were extremely conscious that their pharaohs were, in fact, mortals. Despite that, however, the pharaohs were still revered and given complete control of society; the only ones who were on par with them were the priests in the temples, who communed with the gods and goddesses on a regular basis.

The succession of the pharaohs was usually passed down from father to son, but the royal queens and mothers played a significant role. Preferably, the heir to the throne was passed down to the son born of the pharaoh and his chief royal wife (typically a close blood relative such as a sister, half-sister for example), to ensure a stronger legitimate claim to the crown. Women enjoyed status and importance through their role as a queen and especially as mother of the pharaoh, showcasing her as a symbol of conception and rebirth. Although Hatshepsut is known as the only queen to assume kingship, there were a number of other female rulers although their reigns were typically short.

Only a few of the official succession records have survived, but it appears that the Ptolemaic Period brought forth new changes in the way the kingship was run. One of the most important duties a new pharaoh was given when he initially took the throne was to ensure that the previous pharaoh received the proper funeral rites, allowing the natural order of both the living world and the hereafter to continue. In addition to this, the organization of kingship was malleable

Blake Thomas

enough to support co-regency, where the established pharaoh and his heir would rule together equally.

In the end, the Ancient Egyptian civilization is one of power, mystery and majesty; its culture spread across the entire continent and its people lead fascinating lives, worshipping a number of gods and goddesses, whose stories are no less extraordinary.

In the following chapters, I have described for you a few of the many gods and goddesses of Ancient Egypt, some of the most popular Egyptian myths and a history of a few notable rulers (both male and female) whom we cannot forget. Enjoy!

Chapter 2
The Gods and Goddesses of Ancient Egypt

Egyptian mythology is inundated with a variety of gods, goddesses, spirits and monsters, representing every emotion, situation and location. The majority of the Egyptian deities began as local deities, but they were later on assembled to make a triad or ennead (nine). Throughout ancient Egyptian civilization, there were numerous schools of thought that emerged, each having a lasting impact on society and their religious beliefs, each asserting its supremacy over the rest. Many of the pharaohs would promote the main local deity to a chief national deity; one example of this was the god Amun who was a native god of Thebes but then rose to preeminence as a chief national god when the pharaoh moved power to Thebes.

Numerous gods and goddesses are given similar characteristics and titles at various points in Egyptian history. One example of this can be found in the goddess Sekhmet. This lion-headed goddess, native to Memphis, was given the title *'the Eye of Ra',* along with Tefnut, Hathor and Mut, and was considered to be the protector of the sun god, Ra. When we look at the god Horus we see various deities sharing this name – Horus the Elder was believed to have been the husband of Hathor, whilst Horus the Younger was believed to be the offspring of

Osiris and Isis. Over the course of 3,000 years, the Egyptian religious system constantly developed, expanding and including foreign deities, creating an extremely complex pantheon of gods and goddesses that intersected with one another.

During the pre-dynastic period, the belief system of the region was mainly animalistic. They believed that particular animals, geological features and plant-life to be the dwellings of spirits. As they went forward into the dynastic period, the gods of the Egyptians were portrayed with symbolic animals, or animal features, founded on the perception of the function or quality of the individual creature. For example, the God of Death and Funerals, Anubis is portrayed as having a jackal's head. Real jackals were typically seen on the desert borders where the dead were buried. As such, the Egyptians came to believe that the jackals were safeguarding the souls of the dead.

Water gods (Hapi and Aunket, for instance) were incredibly popular deities that were worshipped by the ancient Egyptian. The ancient Egyptians revered the element of water; the flooding and inundation of the River Nile was necessary for them to survive.

As the centuries passed, the ancient deities lost more of the symbolic nature and began to be portrayed as more human looking, as well as increasing in number. Deities representing various aspects of the cosmos, hunting and war began to make an appearance.

Even when the Pharaoh Akhenaten, known as the Heretic King, established the cult of the Aten, the land of Egypt was not completely monotheistic. In his capital city, the pharaoh proclaimed that the worship of the Atis bull would continue and even then, statues of the god of childbirth, the dwarf Bes, have been discovered. In addition to this, Akhenaten and his wife, the renowned beauty Nefertiti, were regularly equated to Shu and Tefnut. This illustrates the fact that aspects of the old religion were not completely wiped out even with the establishment of a new one god. Later on, when Christianity was established to the land, many of the iconic symbols and legends of the ancient period were adapted and modified to suit the Christians new canon.

In this next section we will look at some of the gods and goddesses of ancient Egypt to understand the role they played in society and history. Do keep in mind that the number of gods and goddesses the Egyptians worshipped were innumerous; I've listed only a handful of them here.

Amaunet

Amaunet is an ancient goddess of the air or wind. Her name translates as 'She Who is Hidden', 'The Invisible One' or 'That Which is Concealed', emphasizing her role as an atmospheric deity. Amaunet is one of eight primordial deities who existed before the world was created and together they formed the elemental ocean. Ancient Egyptian mythology has numerous creation stories that came out of different locations, usually featuring the local god as the main deity in the myth. Amaunet's creation myth originates in the town of Khmum near Thebes, which was widely known as

Hermopolis ('City of Hermes' in Greek). The Greeks connected the chief local god of Djehuty, better known with the Greek name Thoth, with the town. The name of the town, Khmun, translates as Eight Town, and even today's contemporary name of el-Ashmunein, originates from the Coptic word for eight. The number eight was an important figure as it emphasized the significance of totality and the Ogdoad of the region gave the town its name.

The local creation myth from Khmum tells that the primordial ocean consisted of four elements which were symbolized by two pairs of male and female divinities; Formlessness was symbolized by Heh and Hauhet; Darkness by Kek and Kauket; Water by Nun and Naunet; and Air (or Hidden Power) by Amun and

Amaunet. Through these gods and goddesses, the primordial waters flowed until they rushed together so violently that they caused flames to rise up and fashion the primordial mound, known as the Isle of Fire.

Thoth, the scribe god and a moon deity, arrived on the mound in the shape of an ibis bird and produced an egg. From the egg, the sun was born and Time began. All the gods except for Amun departed to live in the underworld.

The local inhabitants of the town state that this version is the earliest creation myth and that Khmum was the locality of the legendary Isle of Fire.

The primordial ocean is a symbol of the yearly flooding and inundation of the River Nile, which has everything required to create the world, and from which the eight gods discovered the complete vitality within the chaotic nature.

Although Amaunet's name is clearly the feminine form of Amun, she appears at the same time as he did. The earliest reference of both deities is together in a Pyramid Text dated to around 2350 – 2345 BCE, in the Fifth Dynasty. The Pyramid Texts are a collection of spells inscribed in the walls of the burial chambers in the pyramids, on the understanding that they would safeguard the pharaoh as he made his way into the hereafter. Although they date back to the Fifth Dynasty, it is highly likely that they are much older, particularly because they us an archaic form of language. Amaunet and Amun, along with the other pairs of gods, were seen to be protective gods, and symbolized the shadowy and veiled powers of nature, which made them ideal gods to protect the deceased pharaoh on his journey.

Just as the other goddesses from the Ogdoad, Amaunet was represented as a woman with a snakehead, although there are illustrations of them with jackal heads instead of feet. The male gods were typically shown with the heads of frogs, as frogs (along with snakes and jackals) are connected with water, the Underworld and change. However, all eight together were sometimes portrayed as baboons, just as Djehuty was occasionally portrayed. Amaunet was occasionally shown in her human guise, wearing the Red Crown of Upper Egypt, occasionally holding a papyrus staff that symbolized the primordial waters in addition as a prosperous new life.

Despite the fact that Amun was combined with the sun god Ra as Amun-Ra and eventually grew into one of the most important gods in the entire country, Amaunet appears to have remained a local goddess in the vicinity of Thebes. After a while, she was replaced by the vulture headed goddess Mut as the wife of Amun, particularly in Thebes, but not entirely. The Egyptians carried on worshipping Amaunet, especially in her cult center of Karnak and in Amun's great temple there was a gigantic statue of her and there were priests dedicated to her service in there.

In the temple of Amun in Djamet (present day Medinet Habu), just across the other side of the River Nile near Luxor, an 18th Dynasty portrayal of Amaunet is shown. This was started by the female pharaoh Hepshepsut during the middle of the 15th century BCE and then carried on by her eventual heir, Thutmoses III. This particular temple highlights the struggle Thutmoses had with his reign and the reign of Hepshepsut's and her legacy. As such, numerous depictions and names have been changed or disfigured in the hope that he could expunge her mark on Egyptian history. One of these depictions shows the goddess Amaunet with Thutmoses III placing an ankh to his lips; she is presented in completely human form wearing an ancient type of dress typical of goddesses, along with the Red Crown of Upper Egypt. The pharaoh wears a similar headdress to that of Amun, associating himself as the goddess' husband. The temple underwent many alterations right into the Ptolemaic period, highlighting the fact that Amaunet continued to be worshipped for centuries. It is estimated that Amaunet was worshipped here for around 2,300 years.

As one of the primordial goddesses, Amaunet was considered to be a protecting Mother Goddess, an essential role in order to keep the balance of the universe in check. She played a significant role in various kingship festivals, which included the sed festival, which the pharaoh performed every so often in his reign to replenish his vitality and allowed him to continue to rule in success. Amaunet has sometimes been called the Mother of Ra, and the association between Amun and Ra has made her be seen as the wife and mother of her consort. The pharaoh was often depicted as suckling from the breast of Amaunet, which gave him strength and protection.

Amun

Amun was one of the eight deities that made up the Ogdoad of Hermopolis. He was the male personification of air or the Hidden Power and was the husband of Amaunet. However, in the 12th Dynasty, Amun's worship was established in Thebes and he was given Mut as his wife and became the chief god over the rest. With Mut, Amun had a single child, the moon deity known as Khonsu. The Pharaoh Ahmose I of the New Kingdom era had him promoted to a national god instead of a local one, as the pharaoh believed that Amun had aided him in forcing the Hyksos from Egyptian lands. In addition to this, Amun was also brought into the Ennead of Heliopolis where he was identified with Ra and became known as Amun-Ra.

Although it is possible that there were once two distinct deities given the same name of Amun, it is much more likely that the attributes of the Theban god Montu (also known as Montju) were simply transferred to Amun of Heliopolis when the latter superseded him as the chief deity of the region.

The meaning of Amun's name can be translated as 'the Hidden One' or the 'Secret One'; according to mythology, Amun created himself before creating the rest of the world whilst maintaining distance from the world itself. As such, Amun was the first enigmatic and undividable creator. When he was combined with the sun god Ra, he became both a visible and invisible god – this duality would be mirrored later on in much of

Egyptian mythology and the individual identities of the gods.

Amun superseded Montu in Thebes and then the rest of the country, but was also became combined with many other deities, becoming known as Amun-Ra-Atum, Amun-Ra-Montu, Amun-Min and Amun-Ra-Horakhty.

As with many deities in mythology, Amun was linked with various animals, some of which he would take their shape in inscriptions. The first form he was associated with was a goose whereby he was known as the 'Great Cackler'. Legends tell how he could shed his skin just as a snake would and rejuvenate himself. The most common depiction of him in animal form was that of a ram, which symbolizes fertility. Other depictions show him as a human man with a ram's head, a uraeus (Royal

Cobra), and a crocodile head or with the head of an ape. Another common form he takes in inscriptions is that of a king sitting on his throne with the double plumed crown on his head. Throughout the Ptolemaic era, the depictions of the god cast in bronze show him as a human man with a beard, the body of a beetle, four arms, hawk wings, human legs and lion's paws and claws.

In the Pyramid Texts, Amun was said to be the primordial creator deity, a representation of the creative energy of the world. During the 11th Dynasty, Amun gained importance as he superseded Montu as the foremost god of Thebes. As time went on, Amun's recognition as the chief god was associated with the city itself and when the pharaoh Ahmose I was able to force the Hyksos from the country, he presented offerings to Amun for his help. During the Middle Kingdom, the pharaoh and his family erected several temples to the god, the most important of which where the Great Temple of Karnak and the Luxor Temple.

In the New Kingdom period, Amun had achieved such importance and prestige that the country was nearly a monotheistic culture already. As Amun-Ra, he was seen to be the father of Egypt and the guardian of the king himself. Royal women in Thebes held status and power, and linked with the cult of the god. The chief wife of Ahmose I, Queen Ahmose Nefertari, was given the epithet of God's Wife of Amun; afterwards, this moniker was applied to every chief royal wife to honor her position within the national cult of Amun. The female pharaoh Hatshepsut even claimed that Amun had taken on the form of the pharaoh Thuthmoses II (her father) laid with her mother and conceived her. As such, this assertion allowed her to proclaim she was the rightful heir to the throne since she was the child of Amun.

Amun's will and wishes could be communicated through his oracles that were controlled by the priests. These priests amassed so much land that they matched the supremacy of the pharaoh himself. When Amenhotep III came to power, he created several reforms when he became concerned that the priests at Thebes were holding far too much power but it was his son, the Heretic King Akhenaten, who pushed further and replaced the worship of Amun with the solar disc, the Aten. He established a new royal city but after his death, his son, Tutankhamn, reinstated the old religion.

Amun's power and prestige was so high that his cult was transferred into other countries, especially into Nubia. Amen-Ra became the chief god of the Napata Kingdom in Nubia by the 25th Dynasty, believing that he originated from north Sudan and even the ancient Greeks deemed him to be the correspondent of Zeus.

Amun's main festival was the Opet where a statue of the god was transported along the River Nile, originating from the Great Temple of Karnak to the Temple of Luxor. This was to honor the god's marriage to Mut (or even Taweret).

Anuket

Anuket was an prehistoric goddess of the cataracts of the River Nile around the area of Abu Island, which was also known as Elephaintine Island in both the classical period and today), located in southern Egypt near the Nubian borders. Apart from when the floodwater was high, the cataracts here prevented boats from travelling further south due to their dangerous nature. Anuket was either the sister or the daughter of the goddess Satet, a river goddess of the First Cataract. Along with the ram god Khnum, both Anuket and Satet form the Elephantine Triad worshipped greatly during the Middle Kingdom period (c. 2040 – 1640 BCE). The gazelle was the animal identified with the goddess and the antelope with Satet.

Anuket's name translates as 'She Who Embraces' or as 'She Who Clasps'. This could be a reference to the precipitous and encompassing embankments of the River Nile located in the region of the First Cataract, which is believed to clasp the river in Anuket's embrace. Another possibility is that her name is a reference to the yearly inundation of the River Nile when the waters would overspill into the meadows near the banks – there are ancient references that say how the floodwater 'embraces' the fields. However, there is a darker theory to her namesake, as it could also be translated as 'She Who Strangles', indicating a dual nature similar to that of Hathor and Sekhmet whose legends tell us how they both went on a murderous rampage – indeed, in Thebes, Anuket was often identified with Hathor.

Although it is not known for certain, it is believed that Anuket originated in Nubia. We know that she was already being worshipped in the Old Kingdom period, but was also being worshipped in Nubia at that point. In the Pre-dynastic period, many of the gods of Egypt had already been established, but the Egyptian borders hadn't been established that far south, so it is quite likely that she was of Nubian origin.

In the Old Kingdom period, Anuket was considered to be the sun god Ra's daughter but by the Middle Kingdom era she had been incorporated into the Elephantine Triad. Initially, it appears as though she was a minor consort of Khnun, with Satet being the chief wife, but then was believed to be their daughter during the New Kingdom era.

Anuket has several attributes as a goddess of the hunt, similar to that of Satet, possibly as they were identified with the different species of antelope in the region they were worshipped. Depictions of Anuket show her as a human woman with a gazelle's head, or rarely as a gazelle entirely. Most common images show her as a human woman wearing a sheath dress with a flat-topped crown decorated with tall feathers (a design believed to be from Nubia itself, thereby confirming her Nubian roots). Occasionally, the headdress would feature a uraeus, the royal cobra placed on headdresses to symbolize Lower Egypt, but with Anuket it is to highlight her royal status, rather than being a geological indication. In her hand, she holds a papyrus scepter to signify power and regeneration, and in the other, an ankh to indicate eternal life, equally fitting for a goddess of the River Nile.

Anuket was the equivalent of the Greek goddess Hestia, the virgin goddess of the home and hearth. However, this can be somewhat confusing since Anuket was a river goddess and more than that, her name of 'Embraces' signifies her as a mother goddess. Indeed, she was considered a divine, motherly protector of the pharaoh and was invoked as such – there are inscriptions that refer to her as Mother of the King. It could be that when she was incorporated into the Elephantine Triad with Khnum and Satet, she was then associated with Hestia. Unfortunately, we are still unclear on this matter.

The goddess's principal cult center was located at Abu Island, close to Aswan, alongside Khnum and Satet. In addition to this, Anuket had a temple dedicated to her on the island of Setet, which is known today as Sehel Island, located roughly two miles upstream of Abu. Anuket was worshiped in the northern area of Nubia close to the Nubian-Egyptian border, and features in the reliefs at the temple to Amun-Ra are Beit el-Wali in Nubia. Rameses II commissioned this temple and although the cult statue of Amun-Ra has long been devastated, the wall paintings have mercifully survived. In addition to this, a statue of the pharaoh with Anuket and Khmun has also endured the long centuries. One of the paintings shows Anuket breastfeeding the pharaoh, which illustrates her divine protection. Another temple in Nubia, located at el-Dakka, dating back to the Ptolemaic period, provides beautiful portrayals of the goddess. Just before the Aswan High Dam was finished in 1971, both temples were disassembled and then reconstructed on elevated ground in order to protect it from being submerged by the waters of the newly created Lake Nassar.

Elephantine Island, or Abu Island, was the capital city in the First Upper Nome (which roughly equates to a province or administrative locality), which has been inhabited as early as the Early Dynastic era (c. 3100 – 2686 BCE). A temple had been erected here on the cataract but as time went on and the amount of land available was limited, later temples were established on each other, so that archaeologists can clearly see the development of construction levels. The original shrine established there was an alcove carved into the rock that was most likely the place where the god's cult statue was positioned – we still do not know the identity of the god worshiped there unfortunately. However, from the archaeological evidence, particularly figurines of children (suggesting that they were ritual offerings in the hopes of a straightforward birth), it is most likely that the deity was a goddess instead of a male god. It is possible that the goddess was Satet, or an early version of her, as she was far more associated with giving birth and would be worshipped there later on.

Elephantine Island receives its name from the ivory trade that ran through this area; as an entrance to Nubia, many excursions (both royal and commercial) were regularly started from this point. The Elephantine Triad was often beseeched by traders, merchants and adventurers in order to gain protection from the precarious voyages they were just about to embark on. Archaeologists have uncovered over 200 inscriptions to Anuket and the other deities on Sehel Island itself, thanking them for their protection to and from the region.

Anuket and Satet have already been mentioned that they could have been sisters or mother and daughter, but another theory is that they were originally one goddess who was then separated into two identities. During the later periods of Dynastic Egypt, the two goddesses were often compared with Isis and Nephthys, sister goddesses, who were known in mythology for the roles in supporting and mourning for Osiris – so it could be that Anuket and Satet were considered to be a local version of Isis and Nephthys.

Anuket was also known as Anket, Anquet, with Anukis being the Greek version of her name. Her titles also include Lady of Elephantine, Lady of the Cataracts, Lady of Heaven and Mistress of Nubia, to name but a few.

Bast

Also known as Bastet, Bast is one of the most well-known and beloved deities from Egyptian mythology. Known popularly as the cat goddess, Bast originally was shown with the head of a lioness or of a dessert sand cat; it was only in the New Kingdom era that she became identified with the domesticated cat. Despite this, her roots as a war-like goddess still remained. She was the divine personification of the liveliness, elegance, warmth and calculating nature of the cat, along with the ferocious strength of a lion. Her main cult center was located at Bubastis in Lower Egypt, in the 18th nome, but she was worshipped throughout the country. At one point in the Late Period, Bubastis became the Egyptian capital and Bast's name was used in various pharaohs' throne names.

The translation of her name is as 'Devouring Lady' but the phonetic aspects of part of the hieroglyphs used are replaced with a different one when it comes to the word 'Devour'. Part of her name is identified with an oil jar, which is connected with perfume – Bast was seen to be the mother of a perfume god, Nefertum, indicating that although she may be sweet and beautiful, she was a dangerous predator at heart.

In art, Bast was often portrayed as a human woman with the head of a lioness, desert sand cat or of a domesticated cat. In one hand she typically holds an ankh, the symbol of eternal life, or a papyrus wand to signify Lower Egypt. Sporadically, Bast is shown holding a war scepter and surrounded by kittens.

Sekhmet

The prehistoric goddess of war, annihilation, pestilence and healing, Sekhmet is a well-known and popular deity from ancient Egyptian mythology. Her name translates as 'The Powerful One' and has been identified with Hathor in various locations and periods. Typically, she is shown as a human woman with a lioness head, occasionally with a sun disc and uraeus on her headdress. As such, she is the personification of the harsh heat of the sun. Together with her consort Ptah and their son, Nefertum (or sometimes with Imhotep), they make up the Memphis Triad.

Legends tell that the sun god Ra became enraged with humans in earth and so tore out his eye and threw it at the humans. Doing so, the eye transformed into the goddess Sekhmet in her lioness form and she began to kill the humans without mercy, drinking their blood by the gallon. Upon seeing her destructive force, Ra realized that if she continued killing the way she was, there would be no humans left on earth. Ra mixed beer and pomegranate juice together in a lake; Sekhmet, thinking this was an entire lake of blood, drank the entire contents before passing out. The following day when she awoke, she was quieter and humanity was spared.

Although Sekhmet was a destructive and warlike deity, she had a dual nature just as many of the other deities in the Egyptian pantheon. When the people did not worship her appropriately, she could send plagues to ravish the land, but when honored enough, she is able to cure them.

Originally, Sekhmet was the consort of the patron god of artists, Ptah. Together they had a son, Nefertum, but later accounts claim she was the mother of Imhotep, a mortal architect who was deified. Imhotep served three pharaohs in his lifetime but his crowning achievement was the creation of the Step Pyramid, recognized as the first pyramid built in ancient Egypt. When he died, he was proclaimed a god and worshipped as a deity of doctors, being able to cure the sick.

Hathor

The ancient goddess of the sky and the mother of the falcon-headed sun god Horus, Hathor is one of the most iconic deities from ancient Egyptian mythology. Hathor's name translates as 'House of Horus' since the sun is housed in the sky. This goddess is typically depicted as a human woman with the head of a cow, or with bovine features such as cow ears, wearing a sun disc enveloped by long horns.

Hathor was considered to be the goddess of love, music, dance, festivals, beauty and joy. The guardian of women, she was invoked whenever human women enhanced their beauty. Appealing to Hathor could bless a woman with fertility and since many of the items used in her sacred rites (such as the sistrum and the menat necklace) were linked with an erotic nature, she was considered to be the Egyptian equivalent of the Greek goddess Aphrodite.

Hathor was an ancient goddess; legends tell how she rose from the reeds in cow form at the beginning of time when the primordial floodwaters receded. Her annual celebration was held on the 19th of July, considered the first day of the year, and was celebrated at her temple in Dendera. Before the sun rose, her cult statue would be taken to the roof of the temple, and when the sun would touch it, the Egyptians believed that her husband Horus was touching her, representing the sanctified matrimony of both sun and sky.

As with Sekhmet, Hathor was also considered to be a daughter of the sun god Ra and the same legend of

Sekhmet's bloody massacre of mankind is at times transferred to Hathor. At Kom el-Hisn during the Middle Kingdom, a temple dedicated to Sekhmet-Hathor was erected.

Like with many other gods and goddesses from ancient Egypt, Hathor too had a dual nature. In this she was the guardian of both newborn children and the dead. When a baby was born, seven Hathor's would arrive and present the babe with his or her destiny; as a guardian of the dead, she would greet the deceased with bread and beer when they arrived at the Gates of the West.

Hathor was also known as Lady of the Sycamore, the Gold of the Gods and Mistress of Turquoise, to name but a few.

Nun

Nun was the male primordial deity from which all other deities emerged out of his floodwaters. The theology of the Ogdoad tells how the cosmos was created from the contact of eight components, represented by eight deities, of which Nun was one. Legends say that when the world comes to an end, everything would revert back into these primordial waters. Nun had no particular temple or priesthood dedicated to him but the consecrated lakes created in other temples were a representation of him and there are regular references to this in sacred writings.

As a water deity, Nun was found in every water source in the world, including the origins of the river Nile and the annual flooding of its waters. Nun was also connected with the arranging of all the temple foundations, most likely because water will always stay in a horizontal level, somewhat like a modern day spirit level in household tool kits, ensuring that the foundations were always flat.

In addition to being a primordial water deity, Nun was also related with the chaotic powers of the universe. According to mythology, Ra was annoyed with mankind, as they had not been paying him his due respect, so Nun suggested that Ra send his eye (as Sekhmet or Hathor) and do away with humankind. Despite this, Nun had a positive element, shielding Shu and Tefnut from the chaotic powers of the universe, symbolized as demonic serpents. Another legend tells that Nun advised Nut to change into a celestial cow and transport Ra through the sky as he had become elderly and tired.

In art, Nun was often shown as a human man with the head of a frog, or as a complete frog by itself, a form taken on by all of the Ogdoad, but other depictions show him as a human man with blue or green skin wearing a beard – emphasizing his relationship with the River Nile and its fertility. In the form with the blue or green skin, he appears somewhat similar to that of Hapi, the god of the River Nile, and is typically shown standing upright on a solar boat, or else depicted emerging from waters with a palm front – indicating elongated life. Intermittently he is shown as in an androgynous form with prominent breasts.

Nun was often identified with the god Ptah in Memphis where they were merged into the combined god Ptah-Nun. Nun and Ptah were thought to be the father of Ra (or even Atum), but the priests of Thebes claimed that their city was the location where the primordial mound arose when the waters of Nun receded. The Theban priests claimed that although Nun was a powerful force, he was an inactive element until Amun (who was both the patron god of Thebes and one of the Ogdoad as well) transformed himself into the original mound, giving rise to the further gods.

Wadjet

Wadjet is one of the earliest deities from ancient Egypt, with her having an established cult already in the Pre-dynastic Period, but as the centuries passed, she evolved into one of the most important and iconic deities. Initially, she was known as Per-Wadjet from Buto, a local deity, but evolved into the patron goddess of Lower Egypt. When the Pre-dynastic period came to a close, Wadjet was seen to be the actual embodiment of Lower Egypt rather than just a patron goddess, and was typically portrayed in art alongside her sister, Nekhbet, who was the embodiment of Upper Egypt. Together, the sisters symbolized the entire country and were incorporated into the pharaoh's nebty name, which is commonly referred to as the Two Ladies name, signifying that he ruled over both Upper and Lower Egypt. The earliest pharaoh to use the Two Ladies name was Anedjib from the First Dynasty.

According to the Pyramid Texts, Wadjet was accredited with making the original papyrus plant and papyrus swamp. This connection is further supported since the character for papyrus was used in her name and it was the characteristic plant of Lower Egypt.

Another legend tells that Wadjet was the daughter of Atum (later on her father was said to be Ra) and was sent to go searching for Shu and Tefnut when they went missing in Nun's primordial waters. When the gods were finally found, Atum (or Ra) was so overcome with emotion that the tears he cried were transformed into humans. In order to reward Wadjet, he positioned her on his head in the shape of a cobra, so that she could be her father's protector and stay near to him.

Wadjet was one of several goddesses who were ascribed the epithet of 'Eye of Ra'; the other goddesses also presented with it included Bast, Sekhmet, Tefnut and Hathor. Indeed, this title was regularly referred to as 'the Wadjet'; in this guise, her father sent her to earth in order to exact revenge on mankind but she became drunk on human blood and almost annihilated them. Humans were only spared this fate when a massive amount of beer was dyed red with pomegranate juice to look like blood; she drank the liquid, passed out and when she awoke, she had lost her murderous rage.

It has also been put forward that Wadjet was related closely with the principle of justice or balance, otherwise known as *ma'at*. Before Geb took the crown, he had raped his own mother, Tefnut. When he started to take his position as pharaoh and place the uraeus on his head, the cobra straightened up and assaulted both Geb and his entourage. Everyone apart from Geb was killed, although he was wounded greatly. As such, he had obviously upset the balance of ma'at and Wadjet could not let him go without punishment.

Wadjet was seen and referred to as a violent goddess whereas her sister Nekhbet was regarded as a far more motherly figure. However, like the other deities, Wadjet had a dual nature so there were instances where she displays a softer side to her personality. Mythology tells that when Isis gave birth to her son Horus, Wadjet aided Isis in nursing her baby and then hiding them in the marshy swamps of the delta from Set. During childbirth, women would often call upon her in the hopes for an easy birth.

She further helped Horus hide from his uncle and his retinue when the young god grew up, aided by her sister. Horus chased them taking the guise of a sun disc with wings, with Wadjet and her sister in the guise of crowned serpents. As such, when the pharaohs wore a headdress with a Royal Uraeus on it, it symbolized that the gods themselves protected him. During the 18th Dynasty and onwards, the queens of Egypt would position one or two Royal uraeus' to their headdresses to represent the two deities of Upper and Lower Egypt.

Wadjet was identified as the 5th hour of the 5th day every month, along with the month harvests would take place, known as iput-hmt, or Epipi. Her celebrations were held on the tenth day of Mekhir, known as a "the day of going forth of the goddess", and the seventh day of Payni and eighth day of Mesori, the days roughly corresponding with the spring and winter solstices.

Her chief temple, the Temple of Wadjet, was commonly named Pe-Dep, and had been established long before the Old Kingdom period. In addition, the temple was referenced in the Pyramid Texts. Inscriptions and reliefs in her temple show her relationship with Horus. At various locations and periods, Wadjet was the wife of different gods. For example, in Lower Egypt she was the wife of Hapi, and in Thebes she was the wife of Ptah at times.

Unsurprisingly, the cobra was considered Wadjet's sacred animal and was regularly shown in a rearing position, or as a human woman with the red crown of Egypt on her head. She is frequently shown alongside her sister Nekhbet in either serpent or female human firm. However, in the Late Period another animal associated with her was the ichneumon, as it was well known for its ability to kill snakes, along with being the sacred animal of Horus. When a person died, statues of the goddess were stuffed with mummified ichneumon and shrew, and then interred with the human remains. The ichneumon symbolized day, whereas the shrew symbolized night. Other depictions show her as vulture goddess and in her guise as the Eye of Ra she was a human woman with the head of a lion and a solar disc on top with the royal cobra on it.

Chapter 3
Pharaohs and Queens of Egypt

The pharaohs of Ancient Egypt, along with their queens, have inspired artists, historians and the general public since antiquity. Although they were recognized as mortal men, there was a divine element to their nature since they were seen to be the living manifestation, or rather the embodiment, of the divine nature of kingship. Ancient Egyptian history is divided into 31 dynasties with around 170 pharaohs over those 3,000 years. Ideally, the throne was handed from father to son, but throughout the long history this succession to the throne was disrupted by murder, chaos and secretive vanishings.

The ancient pharaohs were considered to be the living manifestations of the gods in heaven, ruling from around 3150 BCE to 30 CE when Egypt was finally conquered by the Roman Empire. When a new line took control, a new 'kingdom', or period, would begin. Pharaohs would often marry their female family members including daughters, sisters, granddaughters, cousins etc. in order to keep the throne within their family line. However, despite this practice, the throne was often taken control by outsiders, fashioning a wonderfully diverse and interesting history.

The word 'pharaoh' is the title used by ancient rulers. It can be translated as 'Great House', and references to the royal estate.

As stated, Egyptian history is divided into 31 accepted dynasties. However, academics are still arguing the different succession lines; it is important to remember that the pharaohs or kings from this era have not been understood very well from the archaeological record. In addition to this, some of the dynasties overlapped with each other during the transitional times.

Narmer

Narmer was an early pharaoh from the First Dynasty in the Early Dynastic Period and is credited with being the first Egyptian king to unite both Upper and Lower Egypt. The famous Narmer Palette discovered by archaeologists depicts him wearing the white crown and striking an enemy on one side; on the other, it shows him wearing the red crown and he oversees his fallen enemies. In official records in the later periods, his name is removed from the king's list but there are numerous references to Narmer despite this.

Menes

The Greek historian Herodotus tells that Menes was the founding pharaoh of the First Dynasty of the Early Dynastic Period. Later historians credit him with the construction of the Memphis walls but the archaeological record disputes this. Contemporary archaeologists associate him with either Narmer or Aha.

Djoser

The period that Djoser ruled over Egypt is one that archaeologists as one of the most important eras in Egyptian history. Under his rule, the country enjoyed great developments in architecture, commerce, arts, religion and agriculture to name but a few. Back then, Djoser was known as Netjerykhet which can be translated as "godlike of body", which mirrors the belief that Djoser was the living manifestation of the god Horus. Although the pharaohs of Egypt were considered to be of divine birth, Djoser was the very first king to be seen as a living god on earth.

The name Djoser and the name as pharaoh Netjerykhet were first associated with each other around a thousand after his reign. Scholars consider that Djoser was the birth name of the pharaoh. His name translates as 'holy one' and he reigned during the Third Dynasty of the Old Kingdom, which commenced in 2650 BCE. There are no official king lists for this period, which can make it somewhat challenging to confirm the pharaoh's rules. It is believed that Djoser reigned somewhere between 19 and 28 years, depending on which resource is referenced.

The family of pharaoh Djoser is somewhat uncertain. We don't know for certain as to when he was born or who precisely he was born to. However, scholars believe that his mother was Queen Nimaathap and his father was pharaoh Khasekhemwy, who was the final king of the Second Dynasty. There are several scholars who think that Djoser's brother Nebka took the throne when their father died and when he died, then Djoser took the crown. Djoser's wife was Queen Hetephernebty, who could be the daughter of his own father. Djoser had no sons but did produce two daughters. When he died,

Sekhemkhet who could have been related to Djoser followed him.

The reign of Djoser is quite interesting and there are many inscriptions noting the key events of his rule. One in particular is the seven year feminine that took place. Whilst sleeping, the pharaoh dreamt that the god Khnum was incredibly upset with how his shrine had lapsed into disarray. Upon waking, Djoser made his way to Elephantine Island and commissioned a new temple to be dedicated to the god. After this, the food crisis was finished.

The archaeological record shows that both pharaoh Djoser and his successors travelled to the Sinai Peninsula in the search for raw materials, in particular, that of copper and turquoise. Djoser was able to expand trade and commerce, as well as establishing a strong civil service organization. In addition to this, the religious structure began to be far more ordered and complex. Scrolls from his reign show that the progression of the arts developed quickly due to its significance.

Djoser's most famous achievement is by far the Step Pyramid, his lasting legacy. Before the Step Pyramid was created, the pharaohs of Egypt had been buried elsewhere but Djoser had his tomb built at Saqqara. The creation of the pyramid was overseen by his vizier, Imhotep, and when it was completed, it would go down in history as the first colossal stone building ever created.

The step pyramid was created in order to ensure that the body of the pharaoh would remain undisturbed during his eternal rest. Despite their best attempts, grave robbers looted the pyramid in ancient times. In 1934, the Egyptologist Jean-Philippe Lauer emptied the burial chamber inside but all that remained of the pharaoh's mummy was a left foot and a few other parts. But regardless of the fact that the Step Pyramid didn't protect his earthly remains, Djoser managed to secure his legacy with numerous achievements that helped his country for thousands of years.

Snefru

Also known as Sneferu, Snefru was the first pharaoh of the Fourth Dynasty of the Old Kingdom Period. His name translates as 'to make beautiful'. He has gone down in Egyptian history as one of the most fair and just monarchs.

It is still unclear as to what the relationships were concerning the pharaohs of the Third and Fourth Dynasties. It is believed that Huni, the final pharaoh of the Third Dynasty, could have been Snefru's father but we do not have any proof that this was so.

We do know that Snefru married Huni's daughter, named Hetepheres. If we believe that Huni was Snefru's father as well, then Snefru married his sister (most likely a half-sister) just as many other pharaohs did throughout history. This practice allowed the new successor to strengthen their right to rule. Khufu, his most famous child and successor, was one of several children Snefru produced. His vizier, Prince Nefermaat, might have been his child as well.

A mastaba (an early type of Egyptian tomb) was found by archaeologists near his Meidum pyramid. It was meant to be for a deceased son of the pharaoh, and scholars believe that the royal capital could have been transferred elsewhere when his son died. Other mastaba tombs for his children were discovered in various locations, allowing us to accumulate a register of his offspring.

Snefru ruled Egypt for a minimum of 24 years and during this period he launched numerous military excursions into Nubia and Libya. His goal was to capture enough slaves to swell his labor force, as well as providing the much needed raw materials for trade and construction, along with cattle. He establishing marine trading routes, probably from Lebanon, for cedar and established mining operations for copper and turquoise in the Sinai.

These expeditions, operations and trading relationships were intended to aid him in his numerous construction projects. In order to accomplish this, he restricted the social organization so that fewer people were needed to grow food. Under his rule, architects acquired the methods needed to construct pyramids.

If Djoser's rule was one of advancement, then Snefru's rule was one of experimentation. Architects learnt different ways of building new styles of pyramids than that of a stepped version, along with new painting styles for the tombs. Archaeologists have discovered paintings in his pyramid with both depictions simply painted onto the plaster itself and others whittled into the walls – perhaps trying to see which method would endure the longest.

Snefru was one of the great builders of ancient Egypt, constructing many buildings but his most famous complexes were his three pyramids. The first pyramid he created was a step pyramid at Meidum but it was transformed into a true pyramid through an exterior smooth layer; this was added later on in his reign and could mirror Ra's importance in the country's religious structure. Each of the pyramids was built with a funerary complex that consisted of courtyards, temples and even a false burial chamber.

When Snefru transferred the royal court to Dahshur, he commissioned the construction of two more pyramids. The Bent Pyramid was the first to be erected. The incline was initially 55 degrees, but the ground underneath was unbalanced and when the monument splintered, the architects had a case built around the bottom. Since the remainder of the pyramid was set at 43 degrees, the pyramid has a distinctive bent appearance.

The Red Pyramid was the third and final pyramid commissioned by Snefru. The middle of the pyramid was fashioned from red limestone, hence its name. Inside, the pyramid's formation is much simpler than that of the Bent Pyramid and archaeologists think there may be hidden chambers inside both pyramids waiting to be explored.

The body of pharaoh Snefru has never been found and we do not know if any of these pyramids were his royal tomb. It is believed that the pharaoh had several smaller pyramids constructed as the locations for his funeral cult – several have been excavated but apart from one, none have been linked to the pharaoh.

Much of the information we have on Snefru originates from his funeral complexes; there are few temples that originate from his rule.

Queen MerNeith

It is still uncertain as to whether or not Queen MerNeith was a ruler of the country in the First Dynasty circa 2920 BCE. She was the wife of Pharaoh Djet and when he died she is thought to have ruled the country but her name does not feature on the official king's list. Her name translates as 'Beloved of Neith'.

When her husband died, her son Den was still too young to take the throne and so she ruled in his stead. This makes Queen MerNeith the first female ruler of the Egyptian civilization. However, it should be stated that various scholars consider her Den's co-regent.

Queen Neithikret

Queen Neithikret gained prominence and power around 2148 – 2144 BCE, in what is known as the transitional period between the Old Kingdom and the First Intermediate Period. She is also known as Nitiqret and Nitocris and although her name is referenced numerous times, she remains a mysterious and unfamiliar queen.

Queen Sobekneferu

Queen Sobekneferu, whose name translates, 'Sobek is the beauty of Ra', ruled the country between 1806 – 1802 BCE in the 12th Dynasty. When her brother-husband, Pharaoh Amenemhat IV, died, she took the throne and ruled by herself. She utilized both masculine and feminine names throughout her reign, perhaps to help lessen the societal disapproval of female monarchs. During her rule, she finished the funerary complex of her brother-husband and commissioned various monuments at Herakleopolis Magna. Statues of the queen missing their heads have been found in the Delta.

Queen Hatshepsut
Queen Hatshepsut, better known as the Pharaoh Hatshepsut, is the best known female pharaoh to come out of Ancient Egypt. She married her half-brother

Thutmose II so that he could strengthen his claim to the throne once their father passed on. His three older brothers died early, which allowed him to become pharaoh.

Hatshepsut desired to rule Egypt and she claimed that she was the co-regent along with her father; she further stated that she was his heir when he died.

In order to strengthen the view that she could rule as effectively as any other male, she wore men's clothing and the iconic false beard, which she had statues made depicting herself in this manner. During her rule, she had her subjects call her King. Throughout her reign she commissioned the construction of numerous structures that have survived into modern times.

Chapter 4
Some Popular Egyptian Myths

Egyptian mythology is fascinating in that it has any number of stories and legends to explain the phenomena of life. Deities were worshipped on the basis of these legends; for instance, the movement of the sun from east to the west was seen as the movement of the Sun God, Ra, traveling from east to west each day. This is why the eastern end of the Nile was revered as the place of birth, where Ra *began* his movement, and the western end was held sacred as the place of death, where his journey came to an *end.*

Remember, though, that there are many versions of the legend that often contradict one another; what I've written is simply the most popular version that has been passed down as an oral tradition.

The Story of Ra and Sekhmet

In the beginning, there was nothing. The nothing was utterly dark and desolate; there only existed a vast expanse of water known as Nun. The waters of Nun flowed together such that they rose to form a small mound. An ibis bird flew straight to the mound and sat on it, laying a single, shining egg that glowed bright, lighting the darkness that surrounded it.

The egg cracked; out came a brilliant, shining light that spread across the entire sky. The creature inside was the sun, Ra, and with his birth, Time began.

Ra was truly magnificent; he was powerful beyond compare. He could take on many forms. The secret to this particular ability was his hidden, secret name that no one except he himself knew; because of this, that which he spoke the name of came into being instantly.

"I am Khepara at the dawn," he announced, and the sun rose on the eastern banks of the Nile for the first time in all of Creation.

"I am Ra at noon," he proclaimed, and the sun moved towards the zenith of the sky, hanging over the Nile for the first time in all of Creation.

"And I am Atum in the dusk," he declared, and the sun set on the western bank of the Nile for the first time in all of Creation.

He named Shu and the winds came into existence, blowing in all directions. He named Tefnut, who was the spitter, and for the first time, rains fell. He called out the name of Geb, and the earth blossomed into being and he declared the name of Nut, who arched over the earth as the sky, with her feet on one horizon and her hands on the other. Ra named Hapi, and the Nile finally flowed through the length of Egypt, bringing Life to the land.

With the gods and goddesses named, Ra moved to the earth, where he named all the things that grow upon it. They bloomed into existence, preening under his attention. He saved mankind for the last; he uttered the name of man and woman, and finally, the land of Egypt was now populated with people who would worship the great Sun God.

But just bringing them to life was not to be the end of Ra's journey; he took the shape of a man and installed himself on the throne of Egypt. Thus, Ra became the first Pharaoh of the land, ruling his subjects with a kind but firm hand for thousands and thousands of years. His rule was fruitful and prosperous; as a god, he gave his people bountiful harvests and feasts, letting them live in such wonder and peace, that the Egyptians spoke millennia later spoke of "all good things that happened in the time of Ra."

But nothing lasts forever, not even the sun.

As a man, Ra grew old. Even he was not exempt to the passage of time; the men began to stop revering him and they started ignoring his orders. He was no longer held in awe or fear and his laws were laughed at.

"Look at the great God Ra!" they jeered, "His bones are brittle as silver, his skin jaundiced like gold and his hair is the color of the lapis lazuli!"

And so it went on, the mocking of Ra.

It did not take long for the Sun God to sit up and take notice. He grew angry at the way the men laughed at him; he raged at the fact that they no longer obeyed his laws or accepted his rule. But most of all, he was utterly disheartened at the evil they committed in his name.

And so he called a council of all the gods he had given life to by naming them. Shu and Tefnut and Geb and Nut all gathered, but Ra also called upon Nun. Mankind knew not what was happening; they carried on their hateful work in Egypt as the gods and goddesses came together in Ra's Secret Palace at the great god's behest.

Ra spoke to Nun and the rest. His voice was a weary, broken record, the strength of it waning as time passed on. "Eldest of the gods," he greeted Nun, "You brought me into existence," and he turned to the others, "And all of you whom I have created..."

"Look now upon mankind, whom I called forth into existence with a glance of my Eye. See now that they plot against me; listen to what they would jeer of me and my name. Once, they revered me. Now, they spit upon my name. Tell me, what must I do of them? For I do not wish to destroy them lest I have heard you counsel."

It was Nun who first answered his plea, "My son, Ra, thou art greater than those whom you made. Turn your mighty Eye upon their insolent lives and let loose destruction amongst them in the form of your daughter, the goddess Sekhmet."

The other gods and goddesses agreed with Nun.

"Let Sekhmet loose upon them and send them the mighty glare of your Eye till they cower in fear!" they all cried and bowed so low in front of Ra that their foreheads began to touch the ground.

And thus, from the terrible glare of Ra's mighty Eye came into being the goddess Sekhmet, fierce and angry. Her chief delight was slaughter and it was in blood that she found the most pleasure. She was a lioness in battle, pouncing upon her prey before it even understood what was happening; there was no one fiercer or more capable of being Ra's protector.

At Ra's bidding, she flew to the Upper and Lower Levels of Egypt. She took to slaying those who scorned the great god; she slit the throats of men who disobeyed his laws and bathed in the blood of those who dared commit evil in his name. She killed those in hiding in the mountains that lay on either side of the Nile and that day; the river flowed red from the blood that she spilt in her father's name.

Ra called to her and she raced to his side; he asked her, "Come, my daughter, tell me. How have you done what I have asked of you?"

Sekhmet's voice was the growl of a lion, ready to pounce after its prey, "As you have commanded and given me life with your Eye, I have extracted vengeance upon mankind and my heart soars in victory."

Ra was pleased with her response and dictated that she return to her duties. She did so, and for many months the waters of the River Nile ran red with the blood she spilt. Sekhmet's paws remained an angry red, her claws curved to sharp points that would tear out the hearts of men from within their chests as she moved from one corner of Egypt to the other.

Sometime afterward, Ra returned to earth to look upon man, who was begging him to show mercy. The people of Egypt regretted that they had doubted the strength of so great a god, and they pleaded with him to forgive them. Although he was still enraged that they had mocked him so, Ra finally agreed to show pity; his heart stirred with love for the man he had created, who now prostrated at his feet humbly as he was always meant to.

But no one could stop Sekhmet, not even Ra himself. She was a force of fury, whose only edict was to maim and to kill – that was how he had created her. For her to cease killing would have to be her own choice; Ra knew well that this would not happen that easily and went about devising a cunning plan to accomplish this task.

"Bring to me swift messengers," he ordered, "Those who will be fast, but silent. Their speed must be equivalent to those of storm winds, but their silence one of shadows."

The messengers arrived as he had commanded and bowed low in front of the sun god, awaiting his instruction.

He said to them, "Go to the Nile, to the place where it flows fiercely over the rocks, into the islands of the First Cataract. Among the isles, seek out the one that has been named Elephantine. Walk upon it and find me the massive store of red ochre that I know lies there."

The messengers took off and followed Ra's instructions; they flew to the spot on the Nile, where the water flowed fiercely over the rock, and then followed the river to where the Isles lay. Among the isles, they found Elephantine, where they came upon the promised store of the crimson-red ochre that they packed up and carried back with them.

They returned to the city of Ra, Heliopolis, where stood tall, proud stone obelisks, reaching towards the sun – they had points of gold that gleamed like the sun, with the sun. However, it was nighttime when they crept into the city; the obelisks were cast in shadows, though their majesty was not any less. The messengers were welcomed into the city with strong brewing beer; Ra had commanded the women of Heliopolis to be ready for their arrival, that they may feast in joy for a mission finished well.

But the beer was not to be used only for that purpose; there was too much for that. In seven thousand jars, the beer stood; ready to be put into use for Ra's plan to stop Sekhmet. The gods also gathered around their leader, awaiting his next command.

"Mix the red-ochre of the Elephantine with the barley-beer," Ra ordered.

And so the barley beer was brought forth and the ochre was mixed into it. In the bright moonlight, it gleamed a strange, malicious scarlet red, thick and powerful, much like the blood of men.

"Take it to where Sekhmet slays her victims at every dawn," Ra commanded his men "Do it while it is still dark so that she does not catch you unawares."

In the dead of that night, the men worked, hard and swift, to trap the bloodthirsty goddess. They carried forth seven thousand jars of blood-red barley-beer – whose other name is 'sleep maker' – mixed with ochre to where Sekhmet tore into her prey. They poured the beer over the ground, covering it fully, so much so that the floor was covered to the depth of nine inches, which is three times the size of a man's palm.

The night passed then and dawn began to paint the sky pink with its long fingers. Sekhmet arrived as promised, licking her lips in anticipation of the prey whose blood she would get to drink this day. But alas! There was no living creature in sight when she arrived; there was only blood, rivers and rivers of it that coated the ground she walked on.

'Twas obviously the red-colored beer, but Sekhmet was not aware of that; the beer looked thick and red and flowed like the blood she herself had spilt. She was overjoyed at the sight of it; she thought it was the blood of all those she had slain that had pooled together, waiting for her to partake of it.

Laughing with joy, she bent down and began to drink it. Her laugh was the fierce growl of a lioness about to partake of her kills; again and again, she drank, drunk on the sweet taste of the beer that she believed was blood.

Mead is hardly without its effects; it was not long before the beer mounted to the angry goddess's brain and she went dizzy, unable to think any more thoughts of death or killing. She was now incapable of slaying any longer and Ra's plan had come into fruition.

She crawled back to where the sun god was awaiting her presence; that day, she had not spilt a single drop of blood or slain a single man.

Ra noticed her reticence; he motioned her closer and let her curl up against him. "You come to me in peace today, my dear," he murmured and she purred instead of yowling and that was how he knew that she was no longer just Sekhmet, the lioness.

He named her Hathor, the goddess whose nature is one of love and desire. The anger turned into love now rushed through her veins; she withdrew from the world of men and Ra decreed that henceforth, women were to drink only with the great power of sweet love.

From then on, all the beer in Heliopolis was colored red in her honor with the red ochre of Elephantine, when a festival was celebrated on the New Year in her name.

The End of Ra's Rule

Ra ruled Egypt for millennia; he was the Pharaoh that everyone revered and prayed to, the one who protected his people and brought them laurels beyond compare. But as time passed, his wisdom lessened and he began to lose his glory. For he was dwelling on earth in the form of a man, and what man's knowledge can compare to a god's?

The time was fast approaching when Ra would retreat from the world of men and leave the younger gods to rule in his place. But this retreat was far off yet, and the younger ones were growing impatient. Ra's rule was weakening and they wanted to take over his throne right away. Unfortunately for them, they had no power over his rule – only Ra could remove himself from the throne he had installed.

The true power behind the throne lay in Ra's Secret Name, which no one but Ra himself knew. The younger gods despaired that not one person could find that name; if they could come to know it, then Ra would no longer be able to reign on earth and they would be able to take over in his absence.

Now of the younger gods that Ra had named and brought into creation, there were Geb and Nut, who had come together to have five children – Osiris, Horus the Elder, Isis, Nephthys and Seth. In the tradition of Ancient Egypt, Osiris took Isis to be his wife, and Seth married the beautiful Nephthys. Of them all, Isis was the wisest and the most cunning; she wanted her husband to take up the position of Pharaoh in Ra's place.

Isis's wisdom knew no bounds; she was smarter than all those living and she was more cunning than all the dead. She knew all things on earth and on heaven; she knew of the beginning and the end and everything in between. The only thing she did not know, however, was the secret name of Ra, and it was that which she set out now to discover.

Through each cycle of the sunrise and the sunset, Ra grew older and feebler. His journey through the day used to be one of glory and power; now, it was an obligation that he weakly fulfilled. In his chariot, as he passed over the land of Egypt, his old head lolled to one sides, his lips and jaw trembled from old age and his hands shook as he tried to drive the chariot from east to west. Spittle and drool fell from the corner of his mouth, just as very old men are often wont to do.

Now a few drops of this spittle fell on to the earth, where it turned into mud. This mud Isis came upon and took into her own hands. She kneaded it together as though it was little more than dough, and from it, she fashioned a great and powerful serpent – the very first cobra, the uraeus. From then on, it would be the symbol of power that would be worn by the Pharaoh and his queens.

This first cobra Isis took and placed on the road that Ra used each day to move through his kingdom. The snake blended into the dunes, disappearing amongst the dust by the side of the road so that no one but Isis knew that it lay there. When the great Sun God passed by the road, the cobra reared up and struck swiftly – its poison made its venomous way through Ra's veins, even as the creature melted into the grass and vanished.

The bitter thrum of venom running through his body had Ra crying out his anguish and pain to the horizon; the scream echoed in the heavens and the earth, moving from the eastern end of the Egypt to the western end, shaking all in its wake. All the gods rushed to their ruler, gathering around him in concern.

"What is it!" they cried, "What ails you?"

Ra tried to answer them, but not a word passed through his lips; his entire being trembled, his limbs shook and pain overtook him. The poison, insidious and angry, spread across his body even as the Nile spreads her inundation all across Egypt. Ra reached out to the gods with a shaky hand and then mumbled his answer.

"He-help me," he stammered, breathing heavily, "You gods... whom I have created... I have been hurt... I created all-all things...yet, I-I do know not... not know what has hurt me... it is a pain such as which I have never felt before..." he peered at the anxious gods and goddesses in front of him, "Yet... yet, who can hurt me...? No one knows... no one knows my Secret Name, hidden away safe in my heart, guarding my power and protecting me against any magic..."

With a loud groan, he held a hand to his chest, and then continued, "But... but still... as I passed through the lands I made... something...something stung me. I do not know what it is; it is like fire, but is not fire...it-it is like water, but is not water... I burn, but I then I shiver and all my limbs ache..."

His gaze cleared, but sweat beaded his brow as he commanded the assembly, "Call forth all the gods who have skill in the healing arts! Call those whose wisdom surpasses the heavens, whose knowledge of magic may yet bring me relief!"

As he asked, all the gods came to Ra, lamenting the sight of their beloved ruler in so weak a state. Isis was amongst them; her healing powers were a thing of legend, her magic one of power. She breathes the breath of life itself and it is she who knows the words to revive those who are on the cusp of death. She drew close to Ra, and whispered in his ear.

"What is it that ails you, my father?" she murmured, "Has a creature stung you? Has a snake of your own creation bitten you? Tell me, for I will drive it out of Egypt by the magic that you named me with. I will make it shiver in fear and then strike it down even as it dared strike you."

Fond of Isis, Ra told her, "I was walking by my usual road through the two lands of Egypt, child," he patted her hand, "And I was looking with delight upon all that I had created with my own power. I did not see the snake when it bit me; I only know for certain that I did not create the wretched thing."

"Now," he sighed, "Now I burn, as though fire were running along my skin, and then I shiver, as though ice was running in my veins. The sweat beads against my brow as though I were a lowly man working in the fields on a hot summer's day."

Isis leaned in and murmured soothingly, "Tell me, father," she whispered sweetly, "Tell me your Secret Name. Only with that name can I cure you of your ailment."

Ra looked aghast, shaking his head. "I shall tell you all my other names," he said firmly, "Form a spell to cure me with those."

Isis bowed her head in acquiescence and Ra named all names that he was known by.

"I am the Maker of Heaven and Earth," he said, some power returning to his voice at the thought of his titles, "I am the Builder of Mountains and I am the Source from which Waters Spring up throughout the world. I am the Light and I am the Darkness and I am the Creator of the River of Egypt. I am Khepera the dawn, Ra the midnoon and Atum the dusk – I am the Kindler of the Fire that burns in the sky that gives life."

Isis performed the spell but it had no effect – as she knew it would not. These were all names that even mankind knew. Only the Secret Name would free Ra from the poison that thrummed in his veins; she knew that, because she was the one who had made the snake.

She needed the Secret Name, hidden away in his heart.

"Father," she muttered, "You know well that none of these names will work. I need to learn of that which you have not spoken; I need the name that you hide away in the darkest depths of your heart that I may cure the venom that runs towards it even now. Please, father, tell me... tell me the Secret Name, so that I may end your pain once and for all."

Even as she murmured her cunning plea, the poison burned hot in his blood and the next moment, it burned cold, stronger than any fire or ice. Ra cried out in pain, giving in to the inevitable.

"Let the Name of Power, my Secret Name, pass now, from my heart into that of Isis!" he announced, "But before it does... swear to me Isis! Swear to me that you will not tell this precious truth to any other, save for the son of Osiris that you shall bear, whom you shall name Horus. Swear to me that you shall bind him first with such an oath that the name will remain forever trapped inside him and pass on to none other, gods or men! Swear this upon my name!"

Isis swore to do so. "I shall do as you ask, divine father," she declared, binding herself magically to the oath. The moment she took up her vow, the knowledge passed from the heart of Ra into the heart of Isis and she breathed in with new power.

Then she cried out, "By that Name which I now know, let the poison vanish from Ra's veins forever and ever!"

The venom fled his blood instantly, leaving him in peace. But it had not departed alone; with it, his own power was gone, his rule vanished. With a sigh, he left the throne of Egypt upon which he had installed himself and removed himself from the world of man.

And so Ra, the Sun God, retreated to the high heavens henceforth he came. He now travels across the sky in the likeness of the sun, bringing light and life to the world of man. At night, he makes passage across the underworld of Amenti, steering the Boat of Ra through the twelve different sections of the Duat, where there lurk a million dangers. Yet, Ra passes through safely, without any harm being done to his person, for he takes with him all the souls of the dead, who know the correct charms and the prayers that will allow them to pass through without difficulty.

And this is where the practice of painting the scenes of Ra's journey on a dead man's tomb comes from; the Book of the Dead was buried with the Pharaohs as well as the lesser men, so that the knowledge contained within its pages may take them forth safely into the land where the dead dwell in peace.

The Tale of Isis, Osiris and Horus

Before Ra left the Earth to rule in the heavens, he, by nature of his art, came to know that his reign would end at the hands of one of the goddess Nut's children. So he called for her and laid a curse upon her being – she would not be able to bear any child upon any existing day of the year.

Nut was heartbroken; she went to seek the help of the God of Wisdom, the great Thoth, who was Ra's son, who loved her. Thoth knew that once Ra laid a curse, there was no escape. So he sought a way to waylay the curse and work around it; he approached Khonsu, the Moon God and asked him for a game of draughts.

Game and after game the two of them played, the stakes rising ever higher – Thoth was cunning and he knew that he would win, his prowess far greater than that of his opponent. Khonsu's loss grated on him – with each game, he staked his own light as the Moon God, and with each game, he lost more and more of it.

When finally he decided that he had lost enough light, he threw away the game and refused to play anymore. By then, Thoth, who was both wise and cunning, had managed to accumulate all the light that he had won, making five new days that he set between the end of the old year and the beginning of the new. Thus, the year went from three hundred and sixty to three hundred and sixty five days.

The five days were not part of an existing year and on these five days, Nut gave birth to her five children. The first day Osiris came into being, on the second Horus the Elder, on the third Seth, on the fourth Isis and on the fifth and final day was born Nephthys. Ra's curse was thus waylaid – the five gods and goddesses were born on days not part of the year.

At the time of Osiris's birth, on the holiest shrine in the temple at Thebes, was heard a booming voice. The voice proclaimed to a man named Pamyles that Osiris was the good and the mighty, destined to rule men with a kind hand worthy of Ra himself. The voice demanded that Pamyles spread the word among men and attend the Divine Child, as he would be raised amongst men.

Pamyles did as he was bid and Osiris grew up to be a man of glory and honor. When he came of age, he took his eldest sister, Isis to be his wife, as was the Egyptian custom. And his younger brother Seth married their sister Nephthys. Isis, who by her art, knew that Osiris would take over the throne of Ra, arranged for him to do so earlier than it was meant to be – she devised a cunning plan and learnt Ra's Secret Name, following which he retreated to the heavens and Osiris became the undoubted ruler of Egypt.

In Ra's absence, the men had grown wild and unruly; they killed and slaughtered and ate one another. Isis discovered barley and wheat grain and brought them forth to mankind; Osiris taught them to plant seeds and use the inundations cycles of the Nile to keep the land fresh and fertile. He taught them to harvest and thresh the grain, to grind and flour it, to make bread out of it.

Soon, the people of Egypt learnt how to eat bread and cut only the flesh of animals Osiris deemed appropriate; the ruler taught them to live in peace and harmony with each other and with nature. Soon, Osiris left the land to bring such blessings upon the other nations, and in his absence, Isis ruled well and wisely.

But their story was to end soon, for Seth the Evil One envied Osiris his wisdom and power. He hated Isis; the more the people heaped praises upon the royal couple, the more he wanted to do away with them once and for all. Isis, however, was a woman of supreme wisdom and knowledge – she knew of his envy and his hatred, and she kept such a close eye on him that he could do nothing to seize Egypt's throne for himself.

Seth, however, would not be denied. With seventy-two of his wicked followers and Aso, the evil queen of Ethiopia, he obtained the exact measurements of Osiris's body. With these, he had a chest carved out of the most beautiful and rarest woods, such that the chest would fit only the noble ruler. When Osiris returned to the land, he bowed in reverence to his brother and welcomed him home.

He threw a feast in honor of the king. But Osiris did not know that this feast was to be his end, for the other guests were Seth's seventy-two wicked friends. The feast was the greatest as yet seen in Egypt; the food was delicious and mead flowed like water. Osiris, in delight and joy, accepted his brother's hospitality and when his heart was at its gladdest, Seth ordered that the chest be brought in.

The ruler was taken with the beauty of the chest, marveling at the rare woods it was made of, from ebony to cedar, inlaid with ivory and silver and gold.

"I will give this chest to whomever it fits perfectly!" Seth declared, and Osiris, who wanted it more than anything else, waited to see if anyone would fit inside. Seth's friends volunteered as he'd instructed; but none fit inside. One was too tall, the other too short, the third too fat and the fourth too skinny.

At last, Osiris, delighted that no one fit, volunteered. He lay down inside the chest – it fit him exactly.

"The chest is mine!" he declared.

"So it is," Seth hissed, "And it shall be yours forever!"

He banged down the lid, trapping the king inside it. In haste, he and his conspirators nailed it shut and then poured molted lead through all the cracks so that Osiris would never be able to escape.

Thus, on that day, Osiris the man died in the chest. His spirit passed west across the Nile and went into the

Duat, to the Place of Testing, but it could not pass beyond into Amenti, where they dead dwelt in peace. His body was not properly buried and without the correct rites, he was doomed to forever wander.

Seth then took the chest with the body of Osiris and cast it into the Nile. Hapi, the Nile-God realized instantly that this was Osiris and carried it out on to the Great Green Sea, where it was tossed about the waves until it reached the shores of Phoenicia, which is located near the city of Byblos. The tossing of waves threw the chest against the tamarisk tree that grew on the shore – the tree wound its branches around the chest and grew new leaves to make it a fit rest place for the beloved ruler of Egypt. Soon, it became famous throughout the land for its wondrous extranial growth.

It became so famous that the King Malcander and his wife, Queen Astarte, came to the shore to see it. The branches of the tree had bunched together to hide the chest, which held the body of the great Osiris; the King ordered that the tree be cut down and made into a pillar that would hold up his palace. The King's commands were carried out, but none knew that along with the tree, went the body of a god. They did not perceive the true reason for the magnificence of the pillar.

Meanwhile, Egypt was in a state of fear – Isis knew it the moment her husband passed. She also knew that it was Seth who killed him; she had always suspected his evil nature, but Osiris had refused to listen to her and had paid the price. When she felt his spirit leave the world, she fled into the marshes, carrying her baby Horus with her. In the marshes was a small island, where the goddess Buto lived – Isis entrusted her child to her and then let the island loose to float in the ocean so that none would be able to find it.

Then, she set out to find her husband's body; until he was buried with proper rites, his spirit wouldn't find peace in Amenti and forever wait in Duat.

From one end of Egypt to the other went Isis, searching for her dead lover, but of the chest containing Osiris, she could find no trace. Even her magic failed her; she could not use her art to find her husband. At last, she came upon some children who were playing by the riverside; they told her that a chest of such magnificence as the one she sought floated past them and into the Great Green Sea.

Isis blessed the children and descried that they would forever speak words of such wisdom. She then set off in pursuit of the chest, coming upon the shore of Byblos, where she rested, tired from her journey. Just then, some of the maidens who attended Queen Astarte also came down to the shore to bathe. Isis saw them and offered to teach them to plait their hair, which they had never done before.

Soon after, when the maidens returned to the palace, a strange perfume hung about them. The Queen smelt it, marveled at it and their newly plaited hair, asking them how it had come to be. They spoke to her of the wondrous woman who sat by the seashore and taught them to do so and enchanted, Queen Astarte sent for Isis to come to the court. When Isis arrived, she asked that she tend to her children, the Prince Maneros and the baby Dictys, both of whom were ailing and needed protection. The Queen did not know that she was speaking to the greatest goddess in al of Egypt and Isis did not tell her of her identity, instead agreeing to her terms.

Isis tended to the baby Dictys and helped him become strong; she became so fond of him that she wanted to make him immortal. To do this, she burnt away his mortal parts as she flew around him in circles, taking the form of a swallow. The spell would have worked but for the interference of the Queen Astarte, who had been watching Isis in secret and ran into the room when she saw her baby catch fire. The spell broke and Isis emerged into her real form, at last revealing her true identity to the Queen, who cowered in the corner.

Malcander rushed to the aid of his Queen at the sound of her scream, but there was nothing he could do to stop a goddess of Isis's power. The King and Queen offered all treasures of Byblos, but Isis only sought one thing – the magnificent pillar that held the body of her husband. The King had it brought to her immediately; out fell the chest and Isis took it back, returning the pillar to Malcander who decreed it the most sacred object in all of Byblos, for having held the body of a god.

When Isis saw the chest, she flung herself over it, crying out so loudly that the little baby Dictys died at the sound of it. Malcander provided a ship for her and she set sail to Egypt with the chest. The King also sent his son

Maneros along, but the boy's curiosity would prove his undoing – he crept up on the goddess as she opened the lid to look upon her husband. Sensing someone behind her, Isis whirled around; the force of her angry gaze caused him to fall overboard where he drowned in the sea.

The next morning, the ship passed along the Phaedrus River and it strong current veered it off course. In a rage, Isis placed curse so that the stream dried up the very next day, and following this incident, she reached Egypt safely without any more problems. When she came to the marshes, she hid the chest safely there and then hurried out to the floating island where Buto was still guarding Horus.

But fortune was not going to favor Isis; Seth chanced upon the chest. He was out hunting with his dogs in the night as was his favorite tradition, and by the moon's silvery light, he saw the chest of rare woods, inlaid with precious gems and he recognized it instantly. Enraged, he tore open the chest and dragged out the body of Osiris.

He hacked his dead brother into fourteen bits and then, threw the pieces into the Nile where the crocodiles might eat them.

"One cannot destroy a god's body!" he cried into the night, "And yet, I, Seth, have destroyed Osiris once and for all!"

His laughter was evil and it made everyone who heard it tremble in fear.

Now Isis had to look for her husband a second time. But this time, she was not alone – Seth's wife, Nephthys, had abandoned him to accompany her sister, as had Osiris and Nephthys's son, Anubis. Anubis took the form of a jackal and together, the three set out to find the pieces of Osiris's body. When she dove into the Nile, she made her way on a boat made of papyrus; the crocodiles, revering the goddess, stayed away from her as well her husband. Ever since, anyone who travels the Nile on a papyrus boat is safe from the crocodile, who believe that it is Isis searching for her husband still.

Slowly, Isis gathered all fragments of Osiris. Once she had all the pieces, she used her magic art to form the likeness of his body so that the funeral rites could be administered. She had shrines built and priests called forth to complete the ceremonies.

And so, there were thirteen places in Egypt, which were proclaimed to be the final resting place of Osiris. This caused confusion to Seth's troops, who did not know exactly where he should attack to stop Isis.

But Osiris was hacked into fourteen pieces, not thirteen. The final piece had been eaten by impious fish; the fish were forever cursed and hereafter, no Egyptian would ever eat them or even touch them.

Isis, finally, gathered all the pieces together, and then made with her own magic the likeness of the final piece. Together, they made up Osiris's body and the final rites were administered; she had the body embalmed and hidden away in a secret lair that only she knew of.

With his rites administered, the spirit of Osiris passed into Amenti, where it would rule over the dead until the time comes for the last battle in which Horus would slay Seth and give life to Osiris once more.

As Horus grew up under the watchful eye of his mother, the spirit of Osiris visited him daily, teaching him all that a warrior ought to know.

One day, Osiris asked the boy, "What is the noblest thing a man can do?"

Horus answered, "Extract vengeance upon the man who committed evil against his father and his mother."

Osiris, pleased, asked another question, "What animal proves most useful to a warrior, to the avenger when he marches into battle?"

Horus responded, "A horse."

"Surely a lion would be a better choice?" Osiris tested the boy, "It's far more fierce and powerful."

"A lion would be suitable for the man who required aid," Horus answered promptly, "But for the avenger, the horse is best suited, for it can cut off the foe's escape route."

This told Osiris all he needed to know; it was time for Horus to declare war on Seth. He bade his son to gather his army and sail up the Nile, so that an attack could be mounted in the deserts of the south. Horus did as he was ordered; he gathered his forces and prepared to go to war.

Ra himself came down to the earth to offer his aid. Before they set sail, the Sun God drew Horus aside to look into his bright blue eyes. For whoever gazed upon those eyes would be able to see the future reflected within their surfaces. But neither Ra nor Horus knew that Seth was watching; the evil god took the form of a black pig, one with fierce tusks and red eyes, frightening to look at.

Ra gazed into the eyes of Horus, which were as blue as the Great Green Sea. Behind him, the great black pig passed by and it distracted him; he pointed and cried out, "Look! Never have I seen a pig so big or fierce!"

And Horus turned to look; it was a mistake, for what he mistook as a boar was Seth himself. Unguarded and unprotected, Seth aimed a blow of fire that hit Horus straight in his eye, vanishing before Horus could respond. The young son of Osiris cried out in pain and it was Ra who took him to a dark room where he could recover.

When he was finally able to see again, he discovered that the Sun God had returned to the sky. But Horus, joyful at his recovered sight, set out for war nonetheless, and his country, sharing in his delighted, bloomed into spring on either side of the riverbanks that he crossed.

The battle raged on for days and nights, Seth and Horus engaging their armies fiercely as they sought dominance over one another. Finally, at Edfu, they clashed for the last time. Seth, taking the form of a massive red hippopotamus, yelled out a curse against Horus and

Isis, "Let there be a raging tempest and a gigantic flood against my enemies!"

Storms broke out instantly; the wind howled and the water threw them across the seas like they were nothing. But Horus held his own; his boat gleamed in the darkness, its prow shining with the power of the sun.

Opposite them, Seth, still in the form of a massive hippopotamus, stood ready and strong to pounce. Horus, himself in the form of young man of twelve feet height, called up a harpoon that was close to thirty feet in length and had a blade of six feet at its widest width.

Just as Seth opened his mighty jaws to eat Horus's crew when the storms hit, Horus threw his harpoon. It went right through the evil god's mouth and buried itself into his brain, leaving him to drop to the bottom of the Nile, dead. With that blow, Horus destroyed the wicked one and avenged his father, Osiris.

The people of Egypt welcomed him as Horus the Avenger and accepted his rule as the Pharaoh. They sang in his praise and celebrated feasts in his honor – he ruled well and wisely, in the act of his father.

But when at last Horus passed from the world of men, he appeared in the assembly of the gods and he was not alone. Seth's spirit also joined him and contended for the rule of the world. None of the gods, not even the wise Thoth, could pass judgment then.

And so even now, the spirits of Horus and Seth still contend for the rule of the world. Egypt saw no more battles, for Osiris rested quietly in the grave unknown to all but Isis. The queen herself was admitted on to the sacred island of Philae, where she passed her days quietly, waiting for her son's return.

And now, Egyptians still believe that Horus and Seth will one day return to have their final battle in which Horus will defeat the evil Seth once and for all.

When Seth is destroyed forever, Osiris shall rise again from the dead, bringing with him the souls of all the faithful followers whom he deems worthy of his presence.

It is for this reason that the practice of embalming was considered sacred among the Egyptians. The bodies were set away beneath the pyramids, buried deep into the tombs of the western Thebes. This way, when the blessed and chosen souls return from Amenti to the land of the living, they will be able to find their way again.

And thus, the good times will return to Egypt and the people will live fruitful, happy and prosperous lives under the kind and generous rule of the great King Osiris, his loyal Queen Isis and their warrior son, Horus the Avenger.

Blake Thomas

Conclusion

The world of Ancient Egypt is unlike that of any other civilization known us. For more than three thousand years, it dominated much of the North African and Mesopotamian region. Her rich religious structure and mythology have inspired artists from all periods, providing us with a unique way of glimpsing into this era.

The history of ancient Egypt is just as rich and inspiring as her religious structure. From the Pre-Dynastic period, shrouded in mystery and obscure legend, to the

Blake Thomas

colorful end when she was finally conquered by the Roman Empire, the history of this country continues to fascinate and appeal to all ages.

134

Printed in Great Britain
by Amazon